ACCIDENTS
AND
TRAGEDIES

ACCIDENTS
AND
TRAGEDIES

ALBERT BABCOCK

CITI OF
BOOKS

CITIOFBOOKS, INC.
3736 Eubank NE Suite A1
Albuquerque, NM 871113579
www.citiofbooks.com
Hotline: 1 (877) 3892759
Fax: 1 (505) 9307244

Ordering Information:

Quantity sales. Special discounts are available on quantity purchases by corporations, associations, and others. For details, contact the publisher at the address above.

Printed in the United States of America.

ISBN13:   Softcover   978-1-963209-84-6
               eBook   978-1-963209-85-3

Library of Congress Control Number: 2024904376

TRAGIC HAPPENS GOD SEES ALL

When a person is least expecting, the weirdest
things happen, in life. It's mostly the unseen
things happen so quickly to a person. There was
a person that was using a skilsaw and accidentally
cut his fingers off. There was a one that
happen when an airplane landed in the ocean. No one
knew that was going to happen. Then what damage
it done the Families involved of the lost ones.

When people get shot is another example of how, one
knowing that is going to happen. That is where kids
are involved at school. They say to themselves
what did we do wrong to deserve this problem.
I always said It was the Shooter that had the
problem not the kids. The Shooter is spoil
child or the parents have no time to teach the
child right from wrong, so not child fault either.

The problem is the mental state the person
is in at the time. Another thing was
the child abused or not paid attention
to his or her needs as the, were grown
up. It does a drumroll on everyone
in a different way. Some people can be
Very resentful and other can be very
quiet about the whole situation.

1

It seems how careful you are there
is a something that pops up out of the
ordinary. A person can be walking or talking
and something can just happen out of the nowhere.
This is why you have to take in considerations
how it is going to evicate your life. One
things like a sudden death in the family. What
can you do but accept it as life must go on.

There was a man went to work one day.
His job was a highliner on power jobs.
This day he climbed a pole to fix a wire
and the guy on the ground did not hook up
the ground wire and he ended up dead
from the high voltage lines. This was a
unseen accident.

There was a man that worked on an oil
field project. The man was swamping for a hoe
track hoe and the track hoe touch the power
wire and broke wire and the voltage went
through the ground and the man lost both
of his heels of his feet. Just an unseen
accident which could of being corrected.

Then there as another unseen thing happened.
It was one dark night when a man had a
problem. The problem was the man had a straw
stack on the farm. In which he had a few
Sows and piglets living in the straw stack.
Anyway the man had a few black bears come
in the yard to the straw stack. The bears
would come and eat the piglets then try
and leave.

Well that did not happen the bears leaving
because the man had a shotgun and shot in the straw
stack. The man would end up killing the bear,
and the removing the next morning, with his sons help.
Then it could be a week or two then another
bear would show up and do the same thing.
wait until he seen a movement in the straw
stack and aim for the movement and shot, the
bear.

One night something else came to visit the
straw stack and it was not a bear. So, like
normal when the piglets started to squeal.
The big movement and the shot came from
the house. The something was removed
and buried in the pasture somewhere.

This is one tragic that happened close to home. It started out as a happy family or mostly happy at the time. This girl not very old at the time this happened. One evening this girl told her parents that she was seeing a young man. Her parents told her she was too young to be dating anyone. The girl was eleven coming Twelve years old.

It end up she went behind the parents back and started seeing this young guy. So, one night this girl and her boyfriend went to the girls house and killed the parents and her younger brother. The boyfriend ended up in the pen, and she ended up in a halfway house for girls.

This is what I call an unseen tragic which should not have happened. The parents should have done something with the girl beforehand. One thing is keeping track of who they are hanging around with.
Then keep tabs on the cellphone they use by checking daily who they talk to.
Then ask questions what the age is where does he or she live and what are the parents phone number.

Then there was a guy that had a girlfriend and was dating for a while. The guy uses to play guitar and sing and very good at it plus played in a ban. But the problem was the girl found out that he stilled lived with his parents. The next you know that Saturday the girl broke up with him. The guy took it so hard because he loved her very much.

So, Sunday morning the guy's parents went to church, and then went to visit a neighbor. The guy was so depressed about the night before what had happened. Apparently, the guy took his guitar and the twenty-two out to a stump where he uses to practice playing his guitar.

The guy apparently played the song he had wrote for his girlfriend. After the song he played he put the song he wrote in the strings of the guitar. Then took the twenty-two and shot himself in the head. When his parent eventually came home the dad went looking for his son. The dad found him the same place where he practice playing his guitar. The dad knew his son was depressed but did not think he would take his life. Unseen Tragic.

Then of course there always unseen things
happen. A man was drunk and driving home
when it happened. The man drove into the back
of a car which the other driver was changing a
flat tire. The impact of the hit drove the
car on top of the other driver. The other driver
seen the man under the car and his adrenalin was
high by then.

The driver picks up the front of the car and pulled
the other man out from under the car.
The drunk apologized and help change tire
for him and then parted. The man stops
drinking and driving only drank at home.

This is an unseen accident that happen in broad
daylight. A man worked for a farmer doing some
baling with a round baler. This was a new product
That came on the market. The man made Three
or four bales fine. The next bale was the unseen
problem that happened. On the field there
were a few roots from trees that were
cut down a few years before.

Therefore, a root got into the baler and was
stuck between the belts on the round baler.
The man stuck his hand in between the belts
to remove the root. The man never shut the pto
off on the tractor and the belts sucked the
arm up to his elbow. The man couldn't remove
the root on his arm and hand.

The man had to stand there until his
arm burned off then he went and shut
the tractor off. Then the man drove
himself to the hospital with his arm and hand.
The doctor cleaned his burned arm and
sent him home. The doctor could not
attach the arm back on.
A careless unseen accident.

Then there was a case that was unseen.
There was a man that worked all day then
went to the bar and got drunk each day.
The man would come home and beat on his
wife then go to sleep. This problem happened
on a regular basis just about every night.
So one day the wife talked to her son in law
about the problem that kept happening over and
over again.

The wife and son in law made a plan of what
to do to stop this problem. They came up
with the idea when he came home drunk and
beat his wife. Then they waited until
he fell asleep. Then they waited until
he fell asleep. The son in law brought over
the rifle to shoot him as he slept on
the couch. Then reported it to the city
police what had happened. They both
ended up in jail for some time.
Another unseen accident for the man on
the couch.

Then there was a young boy that had a
accident that just about cost his life.
in the earlier day they had a white powder
called lye used for washing clothes. The
young boy got into the white powder and
had taken a teaspoon full. The young boy
thought it waws sugar but it wasn't.

The lye burnt his tongue and never
swallowed any or he would be dead now.
The whole family thought they had lost
the little boy which was me. That
was a long time ago. Unseen accident
that happened careless on parents' side.

There was a man got up one morning and
went outside. The man was working for a
farmer driving fence posts. This is a simple
job to do until the unseen things happen.
The man drove about Twenty-five or
so fence post by noon. The man and a friend
stopped for dinner. After dinner is when
The unseen accident happened. The man was
operating the post pounder when a piece of the
post broke off.

The post ends up stuck in the man's eye.
The other tractor operator took the man to
the hospital where his eye was removed.
If the piece of post would of went one inch
deeper it would have stuck in his brain
and killed him instantly.

Then there was an unseen accident just about
to happen but caught in time. Anyway in
the fall of the year when a construction worker
was let go for some unknown reason. The worker
was mad at the boss for letting him go. So, one night
the worker on a road construction site put a D8
caterpillar on the tracks. The worker was not
satisfied he also put a grader on the railway tracks.

The machinery was moved off the tracks
early the next morning. No train that night was
Lucky. The guy was caught and charged the
next day.

The next was an accident that happened and
was an unseen event. It was in the fall of
the year when this happened. A man was working
on a road construction site when this accident
happened. The man was setting out flares
to mark the ditches on the new road.
The man was getting a few flares out
of his truck when an impaired driver ran
into him. The impact sent the man about
500 feet from the back of his truck.

When the ramp was notified and came
to the scene the paramedics pronounce him
dead on impact. The driver was charged.

This was another unseen accident that
happened. It was actually on a graduation
night that this took place. The kids went to
a field and had a wiener roast and a few
beer. So, when they were headed back
The accident happened.

The driver was speeding at the time and
the beer was kicking in. Anyway, the driver
hit a pothole on the road and lost control
of the car. The car hit a bridge and killed
everyone inside and that would be a total of five.

There was an unseen event that happened in
a strange place and way. Then one of those fall
accidents but it was not an accident. It was a man
that was hitch hiking when he spotted a farm
house. The man decided to go to the farm
house and get a drink of water. The man got
his water and then stab the couple and daughter
in the house before leaving. The man was
pick up and charged.

There was another unseen accident that
happened. The men involved was some
construction workers. The men went to the
shop for a few drinks at a Christmas party.
There was three people involved in the
accident. When they decided to go home the
snow was deep, and the highway had drifts
on it also. The driver hit a snow drift and
lost control of the car and hit a power pole.

The Impact of hitting the power pole
killed all three people. The impact sound
one person about fifty feet from the accident.
The other two were in the vehicle.
An unseen accident out of everyone's control.

Then there was this unseen tragic that
could have happened. There was a cowboy
moving a herd of cattle down a gravel
road to another pasture. The cowboy
was on a horse back and in his saddle bag holster
he carried his Winchester rifle.

The cowboy said to a friend of his that
he had taken the Winchester out and
pointed it at the impaired driver. The
cowboy thought the car driver was not
going to stop when he seen the cattle.

The cowboy told his friend that if the
car driver was not going to stop he was
going to stop him before he hurt this
animals and himself.

This unseen accident happened so quick
You could lose your head over it.
Well this happened on a Saturday night that
two buddies went for a joy ride. The buddies
started out in on car until they wanted to their
girlfriends places. Then the buddies went to
a place and one buddy got his car with
his girlfriend.

They were drinking of course that night
that this happened. The buddies and their
girlfriends decided it would be fun to
have a car race down the street. So, they
made a plan where this was going to take
place. The street which was no cars or
trucks on the side parked.

Anyway the race was on at a good
high speed. The one buddy lost control
when he hit the curb and landed in a house
across the street. The impact of the accident
did decapitated the boy and girls heads
off. When police came to the scene both
heads were in the back seat of the car.

Then there was another unseen accident that should have never happened. It happened one summer day this accident and not far from the city. There was a young girl going to college and after her classes were done, she decided to go back to the farm. On her way back to the farm is when the accident happened.

At one intersection the young girl got T boned The T boned means she was hit in the center on the driver's side. The professional driver forgot to stop at a stop sign and speed was also a factor in this accident. The young girl was killed on impact and the other driver had bumps and bruises. Both vehicles were totaled.

What happened in this unseen accident was something that should not happen to young people. The use of drugs killed this young girl and just about her boyfriend. The boyfriend was driving a car and hit a bridge. Then he lost control of the vehicle which ended up in a creek passager side down in the water. The seatbelt was jammed and the young girl drowned in the creek. The boyfriend was charged for this accident.

Now this is very serious stuff that happened in
this unseen event that happened. The situation
was that a young man had a drug problem and what
happened was worse. In the afternoon the police
stopped this car and found some drugs in his
possine that was more than personal use.

The young man was a little depressed that
he got caught. The next thing that happened
was he decided to take his family hostage
until he got his drugs back from the police.
Then he asks the police for a car to get
out of town. The police got a bottle of hand
liquor for him and some drugs so he would
release his family from the house.

While this was all happening the police
phone for the sharpshooter from out of the
city. The young man had a shotgun in his
possine that was the worry of the police. The
Sharpshooter was on a roof top when he
saw the young man in the bathroom. The
Sharpshooter was given the green light
to take him out. The police said he that
himself but the shot gun was in the bedroom
on the bed.

This is an unseen event that happened
in the city. A man worked in a scrape
yard, kind of at least brought stuff there to be
recyclable place. After he was done hauling
scrap he would go to the bar and get
drunk on the money he made.

The man would go home after he had a
few and blamed his wife for something.
Then the fists would follow, and he beat his
wife up just when he got drunk.
The wife told him just do it one more
time and she was going to leave him.

In about two weeks it happened again, so
She told her brother-in-law what was happening.
The brother-in-law came over and seen the
bruises on his sister-in-law's face and arms.
The brother-in-law said we had to do
something about this.

In with about two more week, it happened
again and she phone her brother-in-law up
to come to the house. The brother-in-law
brought his rifle with him and one shell.
While the husband passed out on the

Chesterfield the brother-in-law stuck the
rifle battle against the yellow head and
pulled the trigger. That was the end
of the wife getting beat up over Stupide
Both were charged.

Then there was the unseen event from the
family side unseen. A man got himself into
problems like debt and could not figure a way to
get out. Then one day he had it all figured it
out by doing this but he only hurt his family.

The event that took place was that he would
tell his wife he was going to work on his car.
The man's kids were in school so he knew he
could do this without the kids running into
the garage.

The man figured it was a good time
as any to do this. The first thing was to Sind
a rope that would hold his body weight. Then
The problem now to make a noose to slide on
his neck properly. When the kids came home
their mother told them to tell their dad that
Supper was ready that he was in the
garage. That's how the kids found him.

This was an unseen event that happened
in a bad situation. The young guy worked
in the oil patch for a few months in a
camp job. The event happened one
weekend that the young guy had his
time off from the oil patch job.

The weekend event is when he got a
room from a hotel and then he phoned for
a call girl to his room. The first thing
was to do a trip on something he had
purchased or brought.

Then the second on third trip finished
the young guy off by means of killed him.
Then the call girl left with his money and
the rest of the trips and still today nowhere
to be found.

This happened in happened in the winter time
with an unseen event which end terrible
A young guy was friends with his married
couple. The young guy visited his friend
on a regular base as good friends/
The young guy agreed to take
the man's wife and two daughters to visit-

her mom and dad out of the city of
course. It was bright and sunny day they
left the city to go to her parents' place.
They visited for a few days and then
it was cloudy but calm when they left
back for the city. About halfway back
to the city is when the accident happened.

The weather had changed to blowing snow
and a light blizzard condition. Then in a
certain spot it was like a white out that you
could not see two feet a head of you.
The young driver slowed down but that
was too late. A semi driver was pulled over
with four ways flashers going because the driver
lost sight of the road.

The young guy hit the brakes but slide
into the back of a tanker on the passenger
side of his car and killed the lady and
her two daughters. The driver was hospitalize
for a month with head injuries. That's
you call an unseen accident.

Then there was an unseen tragic that
happened to Three young men. The Three
you man worked out of town and one weekend.
It all happened very quickly to the three young
men.

This weekend they had time off work So,
they went to the city. The same goes to a lot
of young guys they say party time. Then when
the weekend was done it was time to go to work.

Then the weekend was a party until
Sunday morning. The driver did not get much
Sleep over the weekend. So, driving back
to work the driver fell asleep behind the
wheel of the car.

The car went in the path of a semi-truck
coming down a hill. The truck driver
never seen the car in time to survive out
of the way. The impact killed the three
young guys and put the truck driver in the hospital.

This was an unseen tragic that happened
on a highway where it was on the side.
A couple of young fellows were traveling on the
highway to a bar. They see this thing a long
side of the highway.

The two young guys went to the hotel
had a few to drink and brought some with
on the way back home the decided to destroy
This thing along the highway by setting
fire to it.

By the way it was a grain elevator on
its way to a new home. The elevator had
to sit there until morning before it
could be moved. Because of safety reasons
like the movers and the public transportations.

The young guys did not realize the
damage it had caused not only the
elevator burn down but the transport wheels
and timbers and the highway was on fire.

That's an unseen stupid accident.

This is an unseen event that happens
too often to young girls. These young
girls get themselves pregnant and carry it
full term. Then they have the baby and
do not know what to do with it. The
young girls have no idea how to look after.

The child does not have a chance in this
world. The new mother's either drowns them
or put them in the dumpster and causes
problem for themselves and the child.
The other problem they are children themselves.

This is a tragedy that happen to often
with young women. The young women
get themselves pregnant and have the children
and raise them up for a few years. Then
they realize that they do not have a life.

The life they should have been an education
with a good job to support a family.
The young ladies make bad mistakes without
realizing it. I" think the young ladies get
depressed and do not know who to talk to.
It is terrible what the children must
go through.

The young ladies either drown the children
in a tub of water or in a lake or
something else to get rid of the problem.
They should not have them if cannot look
after the children's needs.

This is a tragedy that happened at home.
The older fellow had a drinking problem which
means he liked his beer more than anything.
The time was you could buy a beer kit and
make your own beer or wine.

The older fellow one day was not feeling
good. The old fellow went to see a doctor
about his problem in his stomach.
The doctor checked him out and found he
was poisoning himself with the home-made beer.

The doctor told the old fellow to stop drinking
the home-made beer. That the beer was killing
him. The old fellow never listens to the doctor
and he passed away in a month from seeing
the doctor.
This tragedy was a case of not listening
to the doctor.

This is a tragedy that could or would
been a severe accident. It starts out
for the young guy just a farm job.
The young guy was swathing a field of
wheat when he spotted something in the
road off the swather. The young guy took
the tractor out of gear but forgot to shut
the pto off.

He stepped off the back of the tractor
and his cover all's got hooked in the pto
shaft. The young guy had to hold on
to the seat of the tractor until the coverall's
were torn off his body.
Unseen accident careless.

This is a tragedy that should has never
happened. Well, it did happen by not paying
attention to what could happen. The father
of two young sons of his was placed in
a four-wheel drive tractor which was
controlled by a computer in the house.

The operation went fine well as they
where in the field but out of the field
was a different story.

The field was done so the boys decided to take the tractor home for supper. The boys had the tractor on the road but lost control of the tractor and hold the tractor. The boys were thrown through the windshield of the tractor and the tractor rolled over them that impact killed them.

Another farm accident where a farmer was checking his grain bin. The farmer when was close to the ladder decided to climb up and open the lid. He looked inside and was about to close the lid when he lost his balance and fell inside the flax bin. The farmer was trying to get out but every move made him go deeper in. But he failed and suffocated. The neighbor was driving by and seen his truck there running and stop to chat to him but never found him until he empty the bin.

This story happens a long time ago. Another accident which took place on a farm. There was a man in his 50-year-old or about that went to his shop. Once inside he decided to start his tractor. Any way the farmer turn the key on and forgot to check to see if it was out of gear. The farmer put the crank in the front at starts it. The Farmer gave it a spin and it fired up and jumped ahead. The crank when through the farmer killing him.

There was an accident that was on a farm in the late 1800 year. There were two young boys playing in an old wash tub, using it as a boat. Then they used the tub to play in on an old slough or water hole. The play got ruff and pushing started. They youngest one got pushed out of the tub and drowned. Since the older boy could not swim.

Now this accident should not of happened. There was a family that went to a lake for a picnic. The family consisted of 1 girl and 2 boys. Well boys will be boys got excited and wanted to go swimming the girl helped mom get food ready and dad was blowing up the water safety floaties the boys went to swimming. The boys went out swimming and one floaty failed and one boy drowned.

There was a young man that worked out of town. The young man worked five- and half-day Saturday a week. The young man took off home to see his brother who was working out of town also. The young man as told to stay at his dad's place to rest up. But he knew better wanted to spend time with his brother. But he did not make it that night was in a accident that could have claimed his life. He did total his car off.

A case happened in a city where
two women were walking their dog
on the sidewalk. The two women
were sister that was told later.
They were walking down a hill to words
town to do shopping was a beautiful
morning. There was a guy in a
truck that was drunk. The guy hit
one of the women and killed her on the spot.

There was an accident happened
on a Monday morning. The man had
empalsy or fits uncontrol but was a bottle
picker. So, he went on one side of
the highway facing the traffic and went
his usual distance. One his way
back home there was a car with old man.
It turned out the old man lost his
driver's license because of his health.
Not sure if the bottle picker had
once of his seizures and fell in the
ditch or not. But the car driver at
that time had a heart attack and his ear.
Lost the highway and ran over the
bottle picker killing him.

This story happened in the earlier
days. The man was out cutting wood
for the winter. He had a team of horses
that he used to bring the wood home
with. When he done hauling in
from the bush. The next day after
chores like milking cows and feeding
pigs. He decided to cut the wood up.
Then he got the tractor ready pulled
up to saw and put the belt on.
The day was going well until his
shirt sleeve got caught on a branch.

At the same time pushing the
tree to the saw and cut his thumb
just about off. Went to the hospital
got it sew back on.

There was a young lady who was
abused. Then talked into using drugs
by her boyfriend. When she left him
she tried to end the drug stuff. Then
she went to a clinic for help and got
a replacement. She took once a week
until her body was too full of the
meds. Then she passe away.

The incident happened on a farm.
It started out when trucks were
working in the area. The farmer put
speed limits signs on the roadway.
If he seen some one speeding, he
would shoot at the vehicle's tires.
Then was reported and was given
a warning then a few years later
he and his son got into a fight and
end up hitting him in Adams apple
was charged and guns removed
from the house.

This is a very sad story that
happened. There was a couple who
had a baby for three years. Could of
been changed if the grandparents would
of being checking up the family.
Must been a case of laziness for
not seeing the baby and eventually it
die. But the parents were charged
for not giving the baby life support.

This accident happened on a bus trail.
Someone was going in and someone
was coming out. There was no room
to pass just one way. This guy had
picked up his son from school. The guy
got a call to come back to the jobsite.
So, he went back to the roadway in
and someone was going out meet about
halfway head on. The father and son
were killed by the big machine.
No communication to stop the accident.

In life there is so many challenges
in staying alive. Most people have
different strategies in life to cope
with. Most people know.

These kinds of accidents happen so
quick. A young couple were speeding
and had the cruise control on the
car. The hit black ice lost control
and rolled over five times before
stopping on the roof. Ambulance and
police were called out but both
were dead in the car.

Another accident that happened
on a highway. An elder lady was going
to the city to get medicine for her
husband. She turns onto the highway
without looking and a big truck blow
his horn when he saw the car.
The truck ran into her and push
the car into the ditch killing the lady.

A tragic accident happened one
summer. Someone set a building
on fire. But one of the winds come
up and blown a spark onto some
grass. Anyhow it started a thing
called a prairie fire. There was
lots of people fighting fire in the
district so the fire consumed-

a lot of livestock senses. There
also lot of grass burnt. So, then the
fire fighters worked through the night.
The fire truck was speeding down
the road and slipped into the ditch.
The driver lost control of the truck
and rolled and killed the driver.

An accident happen along a highway.
It was close to a city, one after noon.
The car full of people were driving
along and the tail pipe of the car
was dragging. The sparks were
flying and gas tank was leaking.
So, someone got them to pull over
and stop before the car caught on
fire.

In a construction site there was a
accident. That involved two men that
was hurt and killed. When a cable came
loose and hit one man and decapitated
the operator. So, unsafe procedure.

A construction site job was going
well in the morning. After noon
was a different story, that happened.
A man was walking behind a machine
that makes trenches. The trench had
caved in and trapped the man that was
walking behind. The operator put
the machine to back up to clean the
cave in. The trapped man was
killed and the operator seen body
parts on the belt.

An accident happened on a highway
involving a big truck load of pipe
and a car. The big truck put the
signal lights on to turn and slowed
down, to make the turn. The car
came along, was talking to the passenger.
Took his eyes of the highway and then
looked back which was too late.
The car slide under the pipe went through
the windshield and killed both people.

In this place that took place
a really bad situation. There was a
semi-truck and trailer at a certain spot.
Was a sign outside. The sign said
FREE Transportation to a certain country.
But never said that there was no
food or water to drink. So, end up
they had thirty-six people that wanted
a new life. But when they got to
the border. They found thirty-six body all
dead inside the trailer.

In the seas, and oceans, different
kinds of challenges on the water ways.
They must deal with storms, and
wind. There is a problem with
high waves and the creatures that
live in the water. Then there
is always a chance of getting thrown
overboard with the ship shifting.

This was a different kind of
accident. The driver and swamper
was doing a job. When they got
finished they loaded everything that
belongs to the truck. It was a big
truck that had a picker on it.
It was a reverse model the cable
and ball was at the back of the
truck. When driving they hit a
bump in the highway. The cable
came loose and unhooked. Then the
cable started to swing in the
wind. As a truck was passing by
the ball broke the windshield
killing the driver.

In case you were wondering
there is some nasty women and
also men in the world. I think
the cause is the way they were
brought up that has lots to do
with it. Some only value there
own life no one else.

A serious accident that the driver
of the vehicle forgot the rules of
the roads and highways. The driver
was in a hurry so he passed a big truck.
The highway had a solid line on it which
means no passing. Anyway, he was passing
and another big truck was coming and
hit dead on. It killed the driver and
sent his wife to the hospital.

A strange accident happened that
involved a car and pig truck. An elder
lady was on her way to the city. She
was going to pick up medicine for her
husband. She left her town highway and
was distracted and never stopped. There
was a big truck coming and she drove on
front of it. The impact killed her on
the spot total the car off.

A different kind off story. A father was
drinking and smoke cigarettes and went
to bed. His wife was working a night
shift job. But before he went to bed
he was thinking about cooking something to eat.

He turns on the gas stove and
left the room to go to the bathroom.
He just got into the bathroom
when a big explosion happened.
He got outside and forgot about
his sons sleeping. The carbon dioxide
kill the boys then burn up in the
fire.

A farmer was going to the city to load
up stuff on his trailer. Well, the
highway was icy condition and the
old farmer lost control of the truck
and trailer. He ends u hitting another
truck and killed himself and sent
his wife to the hospital with serious
injuries.

This happens very suddenly what
I am going to share. A man walks
into a place with a loaded gun. Then
he kills four people. Then a police
man arrives on the scene and is also
shot. Then he knows he is in trouble
so, he shots himself.

A highway accident that took the life
of a lady. The accident happened about
two o'clock in the afternoon. When
a big truck was travelling down the
highway a tire came apart on the trailer.
There was a car following behind when
the recap came off the tire. With
the speed the recap came through
the windshield killing the Lady.

A father went to work one day.
But forgot to lock the gun case in
the house. The two boys went to
the gun case and got a 9mm gun. They
were playing cowboys and Indians when one
boy had the gun. The boy with the gun
points it at his brother and pulled the
trigger. That shot killed his brother.

A older couple were going on a trip.
They had a trailer (camper) with them.
They got about halfway to where they
were going and camp for the night.
Sometime through the night a stranger
spotted the truck and camper. Anyhow
the stranger broke into the trailer.

Then he killed the old man
first because he was stronger.
Then killed the lady and took the
bodies out and left them there.
Then drove the truck and camper
away. In the end he was caught.

There was a deal of drugs that
went bad. The young man owed a lot
of money. The boss told hired
man to kill him and report back
to him. When he got back
home to find his wife hanging
up with a rope on her neck.

In this case incident happen when
two skidoos were having in a
field. The one skidoo was a head
of the other one. The snow was
blowing from the skidoo. The skidoo
driver never seen the fence in time
and broke one wire but the second
one caught him. Under the chin and
decapitated him.

There was a man went to a
place where there were a few girls.
The man kept coming around after these girls.
Then one day the mothers got together to
talk about what was happening. They decide
they had to do something for this to stop.
When they see this man drive up, they
sent a girl to talk to him as a decoy.
The girl told the man to follow her to
the house that she was alone at home.
The man came inside the home but the
girl was not alone. The mothers came out
of the bedroom grabbed the man and pulled
his pants down. They had a sardine can lid
to remove his balls. After that he never
showed up again.

A man was drinking one day and night
and the next morning. The man was called
to work that day. He figured he was
fine to go to work but had to have
one more drink. Then he left to
go to work but missed his turn.
Ended up hitting a school which
woke him up.

A man at home was loading furniture.
In his truck to take to the city.
The load of furniture was going to
his daughter's place. On his way
to the city was in the wintertime
the highway had black icy on it. The
driver lost control of the trucks and
it rolled over. It ends up in the
ditch on the operates side on its wheels.
The driver was not hurt and was
loading up the furniture when police
arrived on the scene.

One day a man came home and asked
his wife for a divorce. That made her
mad after 20 years of marriage. She
packed her clothes and was going to
her daughters place to stay for a while.
On her way there she lost control
of the car. At that time a lady was
walking alongside the highway which
she hit her. She stopped the car
and was ready to get out when her
car was hit from behind and chain
reaction. Was four car accident.

A man was a heavy drinker in most
days of his life. He got married and
his wife had some babies. As time when
on the babies now kids were school age.
The kids went to school for a few
years until grade six. Then they were
picked upon since there dad was a
drinker. The kids told the parents
what was being said about the family.
One day the father of the kids had
enough what was happening. On a school
morning the father took his gun out and told
hid kids to stay home. He went to the
school yelling to the teachers and principal
that his kids were not treated right.
Then he started shooting at the Teachers,
and principal and students. They were
injured and the police were called
and shot the father.

One Saturday night a man was at
a bar drinking. It was late that night
when he got out of the bar. Maybe he had
to many to drink but was determined
to drive home. After he started the
truck and was just about home.

He was driving a little bit fast|
and blown a front tire on the
truck. He tried stopping and pull
off to the side of the street. Before
he got it stopped he hit a power pole
which ended his life.

A young man came off work one
day decided to take the bus home.
His friend told him he had errands to
get so he could not take him. The
young man went to catch the bus
not far from work. Another young man
was not working but was a chemical
dependency person. He thought the
worker had money on him, and he needed
the money. He asks the worker for money
but got refused, then the other person
took out a knife. He stabbed the worker
and ran away from the bus stop,
The people identified him in a line
up. Then went to court and charged
for murder.

A man came home from work one day
and found another man in his home.
He asked his wife what the man was
doing there. The wife could not explain
why he was there. Then he talked to
his son if he knew what was going on.
The boy said mom made coffee for the
man then he was sent to his room. Then
shortly after the boy came out to get a drink
of water but no one was around. The boy
went to his mom's bedroom and heard
a lot of noises. Then the man took his son
by hand and told him to pack his clothes.
The man did also and then get into
the car and left never to return.

A lady with three small kids and a
husband. They all went out for a
picnic one Sunday afternoon. The kids
had a great time playing in the sand.
Then they had lunch and after they
went playing again. When it was time
to go home the mother told the kids
to put the toys in the car. Then she
put the kids in the car and sat with
her husband to have a smoke.

The oldest boy went into the
drivers' seat and playing around
with the steering wheel and gear
shift. Then the oldest boy pulled
hard on the gear shift and fell into
neutral. The car was parked on a hill
facing the lake. The car ended
up in the lake drowning all
three kids.

A man had a car business which
was doing well in the spot he was
in. He was well respected man in
the town and area.

A man was on road building
site one afternoon. The Forman
as the man of he could do something and he said sure. But when
it come down he was not
sure of himself. He started doing
the job and did not turn out the way
it was supposed to. When the boss
came by and seen the job and ask
him what was he doing. Then the
Forman came and talked to the boss.

The boss told the Forman we
need to replace that operator.
The Forman told him at quitting
time that he was laid off. Then
that night he got up about midnight.
Then he went to the job site and
started up the equipment moving it.
Them moved it into The Railway Track.
Then in the morning the Forman found
the equipment on the tracks and he
was nowhere to be found. They moved
the equipment before the train came.

A young man was working and staying
with his sister and baby. The young
man was helping his sister financial out.
The lady's boyfriend disappeared after
he found out she was having a baby.
Then one night that as everyone
went to bed a stranger came into
the house and killed the brother
first. Then went searching for the
rest of the family killing them also.
They never found who was
the killer or why It happened.

There was a man that had power
over people when asked to speak for
them. Then as time went on, he
was on trips to different places.
The man was leaving his wife at home
on most of the business trips. Then
one day his wife found out what
he was doing. Then instead of
getting exposed to what he was up
to from his wife he contacted a
friend for help. Then the man and
his friend had a meeting and the man
ask his friend to kill his wife. The
man said I will pay you big money for
the job. Then the job was done
and still don't know who did
the job.

There was two brothers that was
drinking one night and got into
some chemicals. Then the next day
there was a house party which
the two brothers were invited to.
Then the two brothers were
drinking again pretty heavy.
The two brothers liked hunting.

The two brothers always carried there hunting knifes with them where ever they went. Then at the party they were pretty drunk and was horsing around with their knives. Then someone asks them to put the knives away before someone got hurt. Well, they didn't like that comment from a older man. Then they start stabbing people that was at the party. Then they left the house and was aways away when the two brothers got into argument. Then the oldest brother stabbed his brother. Then the oldest brother stole a vehicle and was chased down and shot. The oldest brother was dead on arrival to the hospital.

There was a young man got off work on the weekend. He was hitch hiking to where he liked. Then he walk along ways and no ride came along at that time of the night. Then he spotted a house in the country then went to the door and ask for a drink of water.

When the man handed him the
water he took it in one hand. Then
he stabbed the man to death and started
looking for the family. Then he found
his wife and raped her before killing
her. Then off to the other bedroom
looking to see if anyone else was there.
Then he sound the son killed him, then
to the last bedroom where the daughter
was sleeping. He then raped her and
killed her before leaving the house.
The stranger was never found.

A man picked up this girl that he knew.
When she got into the car to go home
after school. The man said he would
take her out for Ice Cream before
he took her home. She told him that
was a very good idea to go for Ice cream.
But in his mind he had other
intentions he wanted to do. Then
he took her out to get Ice cream,
and then took her out to a remote
area. There he raped her the
killed her. Dropped her body in
a remote wood.

Two young boys lived on a farm.
The two boys were brothers that did
everything together. Then one day one
of the brothers was pumping water
into a pai l and had an argument who
was carrying the pail of water.
Then after dinner the older brother was
to wash the dishes. The younger brother
was to wipe the dishes and put them
away. The older brother was washing
the silverware and a knife was putting
down the same time the younger brother
had his hand there and got stabbed
in the wrist.

A man was going back home after
he had no work left from that job he
was doing. He decided to leave his
car at a friend's house and decided
to hitch hike so, he could save money
for his family. The next morning
he went out of the city to start his
journey back home. He got a ride
pretty quick to a small town where
his ride ended. Then he started
walking for aways until he got a ride.

The next ride only took him
to another town which was good
closer to home he said to himself.
Then he start back on the highway
once again. Then shortly after
there was a car coming, but the
driver was drunk. The man was
walking on the side of the highway when
the drunk driver wondered over
the side of the highway. Then the driver
hit the man hitch hiking killing him
on the highway.

What was supposed to be a
good happy day for three girlfriends.
The three girls decided to take a
boat out for a ride in it down
the river. The three girls got into
the boat but had no life jackets on
them. The paddled out quite aways
down the river and things were
going great. Then aways farther
down the river they started rocking
the boat. Then the boat tipped over
and the girls could not swim and
ended up drowning.

There was a nurse from a small town
that ended up working in city hospital.
The nurse was very dedicated to her
work as she was trained to do so. Then
here came along Covid 19 which made
her work stressful. The nurse had
a few patients she was looking after.
Then her patients were getting better
with her help. Then the next few
days the patients were dying from
what the doctor was giving them
as a treatment. Then the nurse found
out the doctor were getting extra money
for each dead patient. The nurse did
quit her job and reported it to the
media.

There was a man hunt that lasted
for a few weeks when a police officer
was shot and killed when he stopped
some men in a stolen vehicle.
When they spotted the vehicle the
chase was at high speed. They
ordered a spike belt across the
highway at one point in order to
stop the vehicle.

A lady was going to be on a
T.V. but before she was
allowed to appear on the show she
was given a Covid 19 needle. Then
as they do in shoe business it takes
time to prep the person before the
cameras. It was about one and a
half hours before she got on the set.
About thirty minutes into the show she
started having chest pains. Was not
long and she passed away with her
heart stopped working.

A young man and co-worker was
talking to each other telling the co-worker
to watch that no one come close to
the semi-truck and trailer. Then the
young man went on the trailer and
climbed on to the heavy equipment.
Then he started it up and let it warm
up for a few minutes. Then the
young man put it into gear to
unload this heavy equipment. The
co-worker had his back to the
machine that was being on loaded.
The machine knocked him down and
ran over him killing him.

A man had a medical problem since
he was a young boy. The man had a
whole bunch of fancy of women what
they would do. Then one day when
he was out and about this girl was walking
home from school. The girl was walking
home with a friend and the man was watching
her from a distance. This was his plan
to watch her for a week or so before he
would do anything. Then the next week
he got brave enough to start talking to her
about her schoolwork and her family. The
girl thought he dressed pretty nice what
she told her girlfriend. She mentioned
that he asked her out to go see a
movie. Then on a Saturday the plan was
able for the girl to go to the movie with
this man. The girl got all dressed up to
go and meet this man to got to the movie.
Then they went to see the movie, then
they were going to a café for pop and pizza.
Then he never took her home but to a
abandoned place rapped her and killed
her and left her body there. Then
he went home. Then someone
found the girl and reported it.

Then the man thought that was
the right thing to so do he get doing
the same thing for forty sometimes
before he was caught.

In the school there were a few
girls was in the gym playing basket-
ball for the school team. Then this one
day an employee was sitting on a chair
watching their girls practicing for a
game coming up to play against another
school. Well, they were playing the
practice game the guy was watching
a certain girl. Then he started talking to
this girl and took her out on a date.
Then got her pregnant which she was
not ready for becoming a mom. Then
her parents took her to get abortion.
Then the guy took a few more girls
out and did the same to them. Same
girls were scared to tell their parents.
Some of them committed suicide.
The guy was caught and was sent
to a mental hospital.

There was a young boy like to work
with his buddy at a job cleaning the yard.
The boys went to the same school and
played there at many different games.
So, they got to be best friends going to
each other's homes. The parents where
really happy they got along together. Then
one day the boys were out helping a guy
to make some spending money. So, the guy
paid the boys and off they went to a store
to buy a pop and bag of chips. Then the one
boy said he was going home because he
was tired. Then the boy went home and
laid on the sofa waiting for mom to
come home to make dinner. The boy
fell asleep what his mother thought
so she made dinner and went over to
wake him up for dinner. Then she
stood over him and called his name
but there was no movement. Then she
shock him and realized he had passed
away. Then she reported it.
The other boy sound out and was
heartbroken that he lost his best
friend.

There was three boys that hang
out together all through the school years.
They were best of friends. They did
most everything together at school.
Most weekend they never hung out
always had chores to do around the farms
when the boys were finished up all
the education they want they went
to work at different jobs in different
places. The one young man decided he
was going to work hard to buy a motorcycle.
So, one day his dream come true
he purchased the bike. Then he rode
the bike for a few days to get used
to it. Then he went and got his bike
license for the bike and was happy.
The next day he was going home to show
his parents and sister his new motorcycle.
Then on his way out of the city was
a circle drive where someone cut him
off. The young man lost control of
the bike and lost his life also.
The young man never made it back
home alive to show his parents his
beautiful bike he worked for.

There was a married couple that was in
the country for a few years that was
retired. They only went to town
once a month for food and drinks. They
were brought up as using wild meat as
there way of living. They also did
a bunch of canning of fish and wild meat.
They always got along together when the
drinks were not available, they played music
and danced had a good time. In the
country they burn wood as a source of heat.
The man would go out and cut wood
for the fire each day that he had to.
Well, he was about to cut out. Well, this
one day he came home and something
happened to him. They still don't know
what he was thinking of doing but the
house was on fire and his wife was
in the house laying on the bed resting.
She smelled smoke and went out of
the bedroom to investigate where she
realized the house was on fire, she
broke the window and crawled out.
He was nowhere to be found until
the next day.

There was a young girl that walked
to school each day because she lived
close to the school. At lunch time she
would go home for lunch and hurry
back to play with the other girls.
Then one day a stranger that just
moved into the neighborhood was|
watching her to go to school and home and
back to school. Then one day the guy
got brave enough and started talking to
her. Then shortly after he invited
her to his place to watch a movie
she liked watching. But she never
told her parents about the man that
invited her to the house. When
she got done watching the movie
she was ready to go home. But
the man grabbed her and forced her
to the bedroom where he rapped
the poor little girl then killed her
and took the body out of town.

www.ingramcontent.com/pod-product-compliance
Lightning Source LLC
Chambersburg PA
CBHW051241120626
46547CB00014B/1746